MATH
ON CALL
Parent Guide

GReaT SoURCe
EDUCATION GROUP
A Houghton Mifflin Company

Acknowledgments

We gratefully acknowledge the following parents who helped make *Math on Call Parent Guide* a reality.

Diane P. Castro
Beverly, MA

Linda Mitropoulos
Reading, MA

Kathy Kellman
Andover, MA

Sue Paro
Winthrop, MA

Writing: Justine Dunn
Editorial: Carol DeBold, Justine Dunn, Susan Rogalski
Design Management: Richard Spencer
Production Management: Evelyn Curley
Design and Production: Bill SMITH STUDIO
Marketing: Lisa Bingen
Illustration: David Bamundo
Part Opener Illustrations: Joe Spooner

CONTENTS

INTRODUCTION

As a parent, you want to do what is best for your child. Sometimes when it comes to helping your child with math, you may not be sure what "best" is. *How much help should I give? What if I don't remember (or recognize) some of the math I learned in school? How can I help my child with tests? How can I make sure that math is interesting and fun rather than frightening to my child? How do I communicate with the teacher?* This booklet will answer these and many more questions you may have as it helps you to use *Math on Call* with your child.

A successful parent often plays many roles in the process of parenting. Let's look at some of the roles you will need to play in order to best help your child learn mathematics.

Tutor

As a tutor, you can help with the practice and memorization that are part of getting a firm grasp on many math topics. You can also help your child learn about math topics he or she may have had trouble understanding at school. *Math on Call* is a handbook which covers all of the topics taught in grades seven and eight and reviews topics from previous grades. For many types of math problems, you will see more than one way to find the answer. For example, **ITEM 035** shows two different ways to round a fraction, that is, give an approximate amount. You should probably start with the way your child was taught at school, but you might find that another way works better.

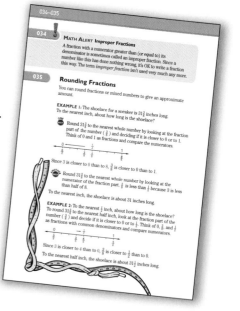

What is the probability that I'll pick the card I need before Mom goes out?

Role Model

Make your child aware of how often you use math in everyday life, whether it is comparing prices in a grocery store, balancing your checkbook, setting up newly-purchased electronic gear, or estimating the price of carpeting for a room in your home. When you need to stop and think about a problem before solving it, share your thinking. Let your child know that some problems are harder than others, and that means spending some time on them and double-checking your work. It also means that solving the problem is even more satisfying. Even if you did not like or succeed in math when you were in school, try to keep your attitude positive. You don't want to accidentally give the impression that it's OK for your child to do poorly in math.

Resource

Some children may be very independent. That is a good thing. Provide the handbook, *Math on Call,* and be sure your child knows you are ready to help.

Partner to the teacher

By the time your child reaches grade seven, he or she will probably have a different teacher for each subject. The math teacher may not know your child as well as the elementary teachers did. Many math teachers teach over one hundred different students each year, so it may take several weeks or even months for the math teacher to really get to know your child. There  may be things you have learned over the years that the teacher doesn't know about your child. For example, your child may learn better by doing an activity than by reading about it in a book, or perhaps your child learns best by listening. It is important to provide the teacher with as much information about your child as you can. It is also important for you to know what is being taught, so that you can reinforce the curriculum at home. A good way to learn about the curriculum is to attend the open house that most schools offer early in the school year. Remember, you and the teacher have the same goal: to help your child learn. Your role as partner to the teacher may be as important as your role as advocate for your child

This booklet will provide you with answers to many of your questions about helping your child with math. The handbook, *Math on Call,* will supply you with everything you need to know about the mathematics taught through grades seven and eight. Together, this booklet and the handbook will give you the tools you need to successfully play the roles of tutor, role model, resource, and partner to the teacher.

Creating a Good Learning
ENVIRONMENT

When it comes to homework, many children need a little encouragement from their parents. Make homework part of your children's regular routine. Help them find the best location in your home for doing their homework. Be sure they have all the tools they need.

Creating a Good Learning
ENVIRONMENT

Q: *When my children come home from school, they need a break. But, after a break, they don't have what it takes to get started again. They often end up doing their homework late at night or not at all. What would you suggest?*

A: When children come home from school, they do need a break. Set a specified time for the break—30 minutes should be long enough. Use a timer if you like. Then help your child get started. Allow short breaks during homework time. A five-minute break every 20 minutes works well.

Homework needs to be part of a routine. It isn't always possible to have exactly the same schedule, because of outside activities, but let your children know that homework time starts, say, 30 minutes after getting home or 10 minutes after dinner. If children wait until late at night to do homework, they usually don't have the level of concentration that they need. Also, since it isn't always easy to predict how long an assignment may take, they may not finish before bedtime. Allowing homework to deprive your child of sleep is not a good idea. If homework seems to be taking too much time, check with your children's teachers about how long it <u>should</u> be taking.

Q: *Where would you recommend my daughter do her homework?*

A: Be sure she has a place that is well lit with lots of room for her to spread out. If possible, she should not be too far away from you, so that you can answer her questions, help her stay focused, and provide help if she needs it. The homework place should be as free from distractions as possible. Your daughter shouldn't be disturbed by the television, instant messaging, the telephone, or other members of the household. Sometimes, you can accomplish this with a soothing music CD and earphones.

Q: *What kinds of supplies should my son have at hand?*

A: Always have a good supply of paper (including graph paper), pencils, a good pencil sharpener, and erasers close at hand. Some assignments may require tools, so have a compass, a protractor, scissors, an inch ruler and a centimeter ruler available. Be sure he has his handbook, *Math on Call*, and a calculator.

A: Your daughter is probably using a calculator at school. A rule of thumb is to use calculators at home as they are used at school. Sometimes the main purpose of your daughter's homework may be to practice computing. For example, she may be learning how to divide decimal numbers. In this case, she should do the assignment without a calculator. You might want to let her use the calculator to check her answers. She can then go back and redo any incorrect exercises.

Math, however, is not all calculations. Sometimes, the main purpose of an assignment is to practice solving non-routine problems. For example, if the computation is messy and the point of the homework is to analyze and graph data, then she should use the calculator. Just be sure she does have the necessary skills to do the computation if she has to. If you're in doubt about when to allow her to use the calculator, check with her teacher for some general guidelines.

There are many items in *Math on Call* that instruct students on using their calculators. Look in the index under *Calculator* for a list of these items.

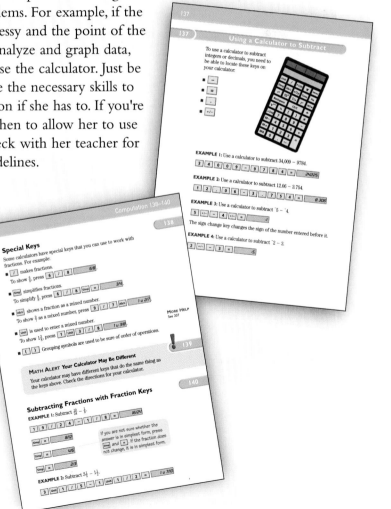

Q: *My son has no textbook. He just gets lots and lots of math worksheets. I'd like to help him review from time to time, or help him study for tests, but I am not even sure what topics he is studying or what topics he has studied. What can I do?*

A: Your son's school should have a curriculum guide listing math topics to be taught in each course. You might want to ask for a copy of this guide. Then, you and your son need to come up with an organized way to keep track of all of his math assignments. If your son has a three-ring binder, he can put all the loose papers in order in the binder. He may prefer to start a special binder or file at home to keep track of the completed and graded assignments.

Some teachers will keep graded homework and classwork in students' folders at school. If your son's teacher does this, ask to borrow the folder and make copies of your child's work. If assignments are sent home for you to sign and return, try to make copies before returning the work to school. If you are really trying to be a tutor for your child, you both need to be able to refer to work he has done in order to choose topics for special study.

Making the Most of
HOMEWORK

Homework is often the most important tool a parent has for assessing a child's progress in math. It provides opportunities for a parent to act as tutor, role model, resource, and partner to the teacher.

Making the Most of
HOMEWORK

Q: *My son doesn't seem to know how to complete homework assignments. How can I help?*

A: The first step is to begin with your son's textbook. Find the pages which cover the topic of the homework. With your child, review the method described in the textbook. Ask him to try to describe the problem and what his sticking points are. This may lead you to suggest that he look up terms in the *Math on Call* glossary, or use the index to locate an item on the topic. The handbook usually shows more than one way to solve the same problem. One of the ways will probably be the one your son used in school. Try that method first, but he may prefer to use one of the other methods. If he likes an alternate method better, be sure to let the teacher know that you and your son agreed that, for him, this method works best.

Seeing a problem solved in different ways may also help him better understand the topic. For example, *Math on Call* shows two different methods you can use to write a fraction in simplest form (See ITEM 037). One of the ways may work better for your son than the other. You may also find the way that matches the method you used in school.

The way you learned to solve similar problems may or may not help your child understand them. Try not to value one method that works over another method that works.

Q: *Some of the terms in my child's textbook were not used when I was in school. How can I help my children when the math is not the same as the math I learned?*

A: You are right. Some of the terms used in math textbooks have changed. Some of the topics are new, too. You will find everything you need to know in *Math on Call*. The best place to start, when you don't know what a word means, is the Glossary of Mathematical Terms (See **ITEM 572**). Let your child see you looking up unfamiliar words—this is a good way to be a role model!

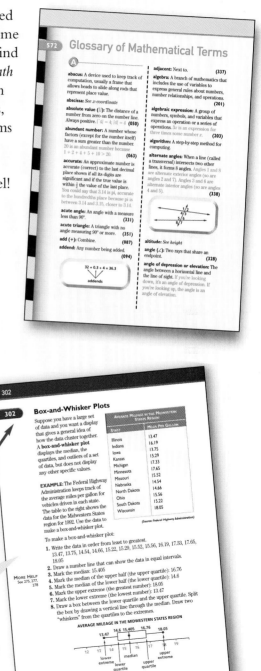

perfect number: A whole number equal to the sum of its factors (excluding the number itself). 6 is a perfect number because $1 + 2 + 3 = 6$. **(062)**

variable: (1) A quantity that changes or that can have different values. (2) A symbol, usually a letter, that can stand for a variable quantity. In $5n$, the variable is n. **(202)**

positive correlation: Two sets of data are positively correlated if, as the numbers in one set tend to increase, the numbers in the other set also tend to increase. **(308)**

box-and-whisker plot: A graph that uses a rectangle to represent the middle 50% of a set of data and "whiskers" at both ends to represent the remainder of the data. **(302)**

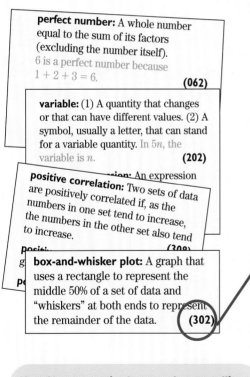

Most Glossary entries have a reference telling you where to go to find out more about that topic. To find out more about box-and-whisker plots, go to ITEM 302 in *Math on Call*.

Q: *How do I actually use the handbook? Should my daughter and I just read it together?*

A: For some topics, looking up the topic and reading about it may be enough. But often you will want to rework the example, step-by-step, with your daughter. You may wish to use a separate piece of paper for each new problem. It is even a good idea to use a different color pencil or marker to show each step. As you work through the example, explain each step. Here is an example from ITEM 061.

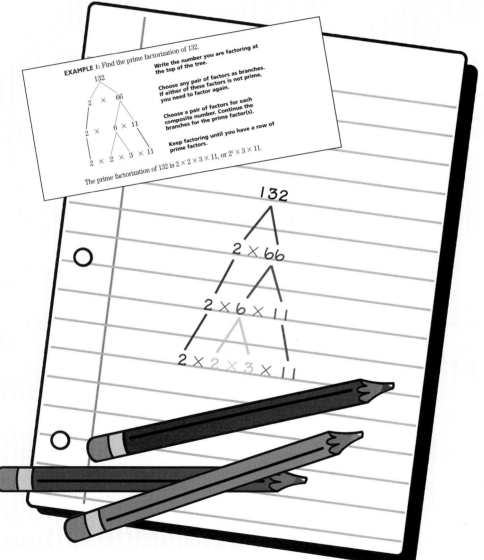

A: Sometimes worksheets can be overwhelming. Try helping him to copy the problems onto another sheet of paper, leaving plenty of room for work. Sometimes having very little on a page can really help a child focus on a particular problem. Copying a problem onto a different piece of paper may also make it easier for your son to refer to examples or instructions that are not on the same side of the homework sheet as the problem. Be sure to encourage him to double-check that he copied it correctly.

If your son is not required to show his work, then be sure he carefully copies his answers in the appropriate spaces on the worksheet. Otherwise, have him submit his work attached to the assignment sheet.

1. $\dfrac{4}{5} - \dfrac{2}{5} = \dfrac{2}{5}$

2. $\dfrac{7}{9} - \dfrac{1}{9} =$

3. $\dfrac{5}{8} - \dfrac{2}{8} =$

Q: *My daughter's work is so sloppy that I sometimes think this causes her to get wrong answers. What can I do?*

A: Try helping your daughter set up her paper before she gets started. Figure out how much space she will need for each problem. Be generous. Fold the paper into sections. If she has difficulty lining up the numbers when computing, try having her use 1-centimeter graph paper or lined paper turned sideways. Also, encourage her to slow down and take the time required for neatness.

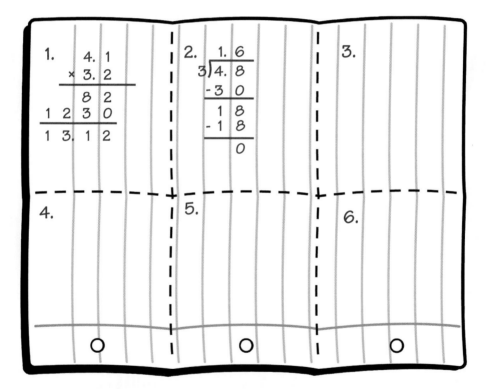

Q: *When my son asks me to check his homework, I find many answers that are wrong. How do I decide whether he has been careless or he does not understand the concepts?*

A: First, praise him for his correct answers. Then, try asking him to redo some of the problems that he got wrong, explaining his work out loud as he goes. If he gets the correct answers this time, he was probably just careless. If he makes the same errors again, he probably does not understand the concept and should go back to his textbook or the handbook for a review. If he successfully uses a method other than the one presented at school, it might be a good idea to send a note to the teacher explaining why he prefers the new method. In mathematics, there are often several good ways to solve the same problem.

I checked the odd-numbered answers in the back of my book. Can you help me check the even-numbered ones?

Q: *Often, my daughter rushes through her math homework and makes an incredible number of careless errors. Then she asks me to find them all! How can I make her more responsible for her own work?*

A: First, try to convince her not to rush. Make sure that you are not accidentally encouraging her to rush by promising a treat as soon as she finishes her homework. When she finishes, don't just tell her which answers are incorrect. Perhaps tell her how many are wrong or which row contains errors. Have her then check to find the incorrect answers. She may slow down and be more careful when she realizes that correcting careless mistakes takes more time than doing careful work in the first place.

Q: *My son says he wants me to help with his homework. But what he really wants is for me to do his homework! How much help should I give?*

A: First, try to decide whether there is some non-math reason for his confusion. If he's overtired, change his homework time. If he wants to be doing something else, schedule that activity away from homework time. If your son doesn't understand how to do the problems at all, take a new piece of paper and do the first one yourself. Use the method shown in the textbook if he has one. Show every step and explain what you are doing as you work. Then, remove the paper and ask your son to redo the same problem on his own homework paper, explaining each step as he goes along. Encourage him to take careful notes.

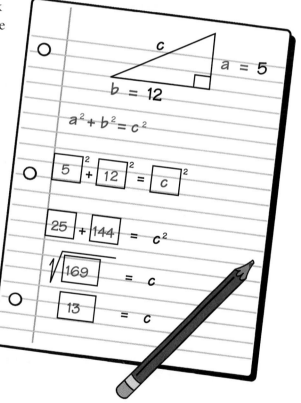

If he is still confused, try writing the problem on another piece of paper, this time leaving out parts of the solution. Have your son fill in the missing numbers. Above all, be patient and work with him, not for him.

If your son just doesn't seem to understand the method shown in the textbook, or wants to see other ways of solving the problem, use the handbook and send a note to the teacher if your son finds an alternate method he likes better. If, after all of this, you are both still stumped, work with your son to write a note to the teacher that clearly explains the problem and promises to complete the assignment as soon as the teacher has provided some help. Include with the note some examples of the work you and your son did.

Q: *My daughter is very independent and really doesn't want my help with her math homework. However, sometimes she thinks she understands the topic, but really she doesn't. What can I do?*

A: Independence can be a very good thing—you want your child to feel confident about her math skills. Don't discourage that. Also, a good goal is to have children completely independent by the start of high school.

Give your daughter *Math on Call*. It is a great resource for parents and teachers, but it is written for students and can certainly be used independently. When your daughter finishes her homework, ask her if you can check it over. Ask her how she solved some of the problems. This can be helpful just to see if she understands the general concept. If she does not want your help finding careless errors, leave this to the teacher. Just be sure she has the basic concepts. If not, send her back to the handbook.

A Mathematics Handbook

Q: *What should I do if my son brings home so much math homework that he is just overwhelmed?*

A: First, be sure that the homework is really intended to be done in one day. Often, teachers give assignments that are to be done over a period of a few days. If that is the case, help your son break the assignment into parts and write down which part he should do each day. *Math on Call* provides suggestions for students who are trying to learn to manage their time. (See ITEM **503**.)

Q: *What if the assignment really is just one day's homework?*

A: First, be sure that your child's social life is not part of the problem. Next, understand that some students take longer to do certain assignments than others. Try cutting the assignment down. Be sure to include a few of each different type of problem. For example, if your son brings home probability and data analysis problems, choose some of each. Then, write a note to the teacher explaining that the assignment was too long for your child and that he will complete the assignment the next night, or over the weekend.

If this is a consistent issue, you may wish to make an appointment for a teacher conference. The two of you can work as partners to make sure your child's homework is useful and can be done in a reasonable amount of time. Do not, however, expect the teacher to modify homework assignments just because your son has too many afterschool activities.

Q: *My daughter never brings home a textbook, just sheets of paper with exercises or problems. She finds it very confusing if I try to help her using a method different from the method she was shown in school. I'd like to at least start with that method, but she often doesn't remember enough to describe it to me.*

A: Suggest that the two of you review her class notes. If these are not useful, refer to ITEMS 496–500 in the handbook for some good note-taking tips.

Perhaps your daughter will be able to recognize the method she used in school when she looks up the topic in the handbook. If not, explain your situation to the teacher. The teacher may be able to have the students complete (and correct) one of each kind of problem on the homework sheet before leaving school. That will show you which method was presented in class.

189

189

Dividing a Whole Number by a Fraction

EXAMPLE: You have 4 pounds of trail mix. You want to put it in bags so that there is $\frac{2}{3}$ pound in each bag. How many bags can you fill?

To solve the problem, you can divide $4 \div \frac{2}{3}$.

ONE WAY You can divide by drawing a picture.

There are six $\frac{2}{3}$s in 4. So, $4 \div \frac{2}{3} = 6$.

ANOTHER WAY You can divide $4 \div \frac{2}{3}$ without drawing a picture.

MORE HELP
See 037, 042, 188

❶ WRITE THE WHOLE NUMBER AS A FRACTION.	❷ MULTIPLY BY THE RECIPROCAL OF THE DIVISOR.	❸ WRITE THE PRODUCT IN SIMPLEST FORM.
$4 \longrightarrow \frac{4}{1}$	$\frac{4}{1} \div \frac{2}{3}$ $\downarrow$ $\frac{4}{1} \times \frac{3}{2} = \frac{12}{2}$	$\frac{12 \div 2}{2 \div 2} = \frac{6}{1} = 6$

Either way, you can fill six $\frac{2}{3}$-pound bags.

You can use what you know about algebra to understand the steps for dividing fractions. Division **expressions** can be written in fraction form. So, $4 \div \frac{2}{3}$ can be written as a **complex fraction**: $4 \div \frac{2}{3} \longrightarrow \frac{4}{\frac{2}{3}}$

You can multiply both the numerator and the denominator by the reciprocal of the denominator.

$\frac{2}{2}$ is just another name for one. Choose $\frac{3}{2}$ to multiply the numerator and denominator because it is the reciprocal of the denominator. If the denominator were $\frac{12}{13}$, you'd choose $\frac{13}{12}$ to multiply the numerator and denominator.

$$\frac{4}{\frac{2}{3}} \times \frac{\frac{3}{2}}{\frac{3}{2}} = \frac{4 \times \frac{3}{2}}{\frac{2}{3} \times \frac{3}{2}} = \frac{4 \times \frac{3}{2}}{\frac{6}{6}} = \frac{4 \times \frac{3}{2}}{1} = 4 \times \frac{3}{2}$$

If your daughter struggles with that method, look at the other methods shown in the handbook. Often, one of the methods provides a visual model that may make the mathematics more meaningful for your daughter.

For example, in ITEMS **189 and 190**, the first method gives a visual model to help students understand what is happening when you divide a whole number by a fraction or a fraction by a whole number. The pictures should help make the concepts more real for your daughter.

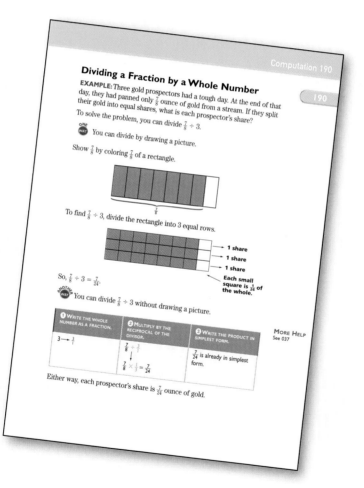

Q: *My daughter does not do well in math. But her teacher never sends home any homework. What should I do?*

A: Ask her teacher to send home the classwork she does in school. If there is a textbook, ask whether your daughter can take that home as well. Go over each type of problem your child has done. Ask her to explain how she got the answer. If she doesn't seem to understand, go first to her textbook. Try explaining what is in the book. If that doesn't seem to work, go to the handbook, *Math on Call*. You may find different ways to get the same answer. One of these other methods may make more sense to you and your daughter. If there is no textbook, you will be able to find all the instruction you need in the handbook.

Helping Your Child Prepare for TESTS

For math tests, one of the hardest things I have to do is keep my parents calm.

Tests can sometimes be stressful for both students and parents. However, tests can also be a valuable resource for students, teachers, and parents. *Math on Call* offers a section on Test-Taking Skills (see ITEMS 524–533), which can help remove some of the stress so your children can do their best.

Helping Your Child Prepare for
TESTS

Q: *What is the best way to help my daughter prepare for a math test?*

A: The best way for you to help your child prepare for math tests is to encourage her to ask questions when she does not understand something. She should also keep up with all her homework assignments. Most of the questions on the test will be just like ones your daughter has seen before.

Encourage your daughter to keep assignments and quizzes in a notebook and try to review them regularly. Regular review and practice will likely be much more helpful than an intense study session just before an important test. During the week before a big test, you might consider making up short practice tests by picking a few problems from each homework assignment.

See ITEMS **524–526** in *Math on Call* for additional tips on helping your child study for tests.

Q: *What do I do when my son does poorly on a test?*

A: Ask the teacher to provide the correct answers if you are unsure about any of them. Go over each problem your son answered incorrectly. If he can solve the problems with no extra help, then he may be having trouble managing his time or concentrating during the test session. If this happens several times, talk with the teacher. Perhaps the two of you can find a way to keep time and anxiety from falsely indicating a poor understanding of the math.

When the math is the difficulty, work with your son, using *Math on Call* as a resource, until he can solve the problems he missed and others like them.

Some teachers allow students to retake tests on which they did poorly. Find out the teacher's policy on this.

You got number four wrong. Try it again and let's see where you goofed.

Q: **What about standardized tests? How can I help my daughter prepare for those?**

A: Standardized tests assess all the math skills your child has learned since she started school. The best preparation is to be sure your daughter is keeping up in her regular math class.

It is not realistic to review all the math your child has been taught right before the standardized tests. What you can do is to make sure your daughter gets a good night's sleep and has a good breakfast before the test. Go over the tips for taking tests that are outlined in ITEM 527 in *Math on Call*. These will help your child perform her best and use her time efficiently.

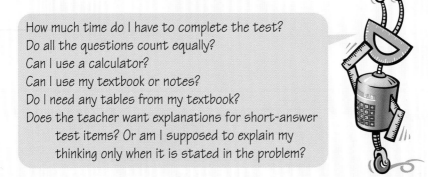

How much time do I have to complete the test?
Do all the questions count equally?
Can I use a calculator?
Can I use my textbook or notes?
Do I need any tables from my textbook?
Does the teacher want explanations for short-answer
    test items? Or am I supposed to explain my
    thinking only when it is stated in the problem?

Be sure your child is prepared for multiple-choice tests. It is important that she realizes that estimating and eliminating obviously wrong answer choices can be very helpful and are *not* cheating. Using these techniques shows a good understanding of math concepts. See ITEM 528 in *Math on Call* for tips on taking multiple-choice tests.

If your child is anxious about standardized tests, ask the teacher to send home some old tests for her to practice on.

Q: *Many tests, including some new standardized tests, ask children to explain their thinking. What is the best way to help my son prepare for these kinds of questions?*

A: The best way to prepare for these kinds of questions is to get your son into the habit of *talking math*. When he has math word problems to do, make a practice of asking questions like *How did you get this answer?* or *Why did you use multiplication?* Ask him to explain every step he took. If the two of you have worked through a problem together, you may wish to model this process by going back over the problem, describing each step you took, and then asking him to try doing the same. For this process, use the same problem, or change the numbers but not the words.

You can find a good sample of an "explain your thinking" problem in ITEM **531** of *Math on Call*.

Please explain how you solved this problem. Why did you decide to test different values?

Q: *My daughter does poorly on tests. She becomes very anxious that she may not have time to finish. So, she spends more time worrying about that than actually doing the problems. What can be done?*

A: If you are talking about routine classroom tests prepared by the teacher, time should not be an issue. Explain the problem to her teacher. Most teachers will allow extra time for students who need it. If your daughter knows she can have as much time as she needs, she may relax and concentrate better. Make sure she understands that she should not pay attention to the finishing times of her classmates.

If you are talking about timed standardized tests, extra time may not be permitted unless your child has a diagnosed learning disability. There are, however, some steps you can take to help your child. Try to obtain copies of tests given in previous years. Time your daughter as she works through these and see how much of the test she is able to finish without panicking. Help her learn to pace herself. If there are 20 problems to be done in 10 minutes, have her think about doing the first ten or so in the first five minutes.

There may be other reasons your daughter is taking a long time to solve each problem:

- Perhaps she needs to brush up on her basic addition, subtraction, multiplication, and division facts.

- She may not be using a calculator even if it is allowed.

- Maybe some problems can be solved in a more efficient way that your daughter is not aware of.

- Some problems require only an approximate answer rather than an exact answer. Using estimation skills on these can help save a great deal of time. Have your daughter look up "Estimation" in the index of *Math on Call* and study some of the pages listed there.

Bringing Math into EVERYDAY LIFE

People remember the math they use. Don't miss out on daily opportunities to help your child use math. Be a good role model for your child. Demonstrate how you use math every day.

Bringing Math into
EVERYDAY LIFE

Q: *What kinds of math questions should I be asking?*

A: Here are some examples of questions that you can ask to make your children aware that math is everywhere. Ideally, your children will soon begin to ask questions themselves. Sometimes you may not know the answer. That's fine. Show your children how you, too, can use *Math on Call* as a resource.

Cooking

- The recipe calls for $3\frac{1}{2}$ cups of flour, but we're making a half-batch. How much flour do we need?

- Our oven runs about 25° hot, so how should I adjust the temperature in the recipe?

- We are putting the pizza in the oven at 1:37. It needs to bake for 15 minutes. What time should we take it out?

The half-cup measure is dirty. Can I use a different measuring cup for the same amount of flour?

Reading the newspaper

- What type of graph is this? What does the graph tell you?

If the price of the car in this ad was discounted 10% last week, then another 10% this week, why can't I say it's been discounted 20%?

- This ad shows some items on sale for 40% off. Do you need to pay more or less than $\frac{1}{2}$ of the original price?

- This headline says that there are 4.5 million people in our city. How would you write that number in numerals?

- What do you think the average high temperature for the week will be?

Grocery shopping

- I need exactly two cups of tomato sauce. Will this 15-ounce can be enough?

- How much do you think these bananas weigh?

- Which eggs are the least expensive?

You'll find that math is everywhere. Once you start thinking that way, you'll be amazed at how many questions will come to you. And remember, if you aren't sure of any of the answers, you and your child can look up the topic in *Math on Call* either right away or when you get home.

This package of cheese weighs sixty-five hundredths of a pound. Is it going to cost more or less than $2.00?

$2.50/ lb.

Q: *My seventh-grade son still doesn't know his multiplication and division facts. Is it time to give up and just let him use a calculator?*

A: Although using a calculator would be very helpful for your son, don't give up yet. There will be many times in school and in everyday life when a calculator will not be allowed or just may not be available. Estimation requires quick recall of facts. Suppose he orders seven pizzas and each one costs $7.98. He'll want to know that $7.98 is about $8.00 and $7 \times 8 = 56$, and that will mean that $56 is a reasonable amount for the order.

That will be $55.86.

That sounds about right.

Make sure your son understands that there are strategies for learning the facts. He does not need to memorize every fact! For example, if he knows $3 \times 8 = 24$, he also knows $8 \times 3 = 24$, $24 \div 3 = 8$, and $24 \div 8 = 3$. If you make a multiplication table to hang on the refrigerator or to use as a breakfast placemat, you can search for patterns for multiplying by 0, 1, 2, and 5. This can make those multiplication facts easy to learn.

Some facts may best be learned by just memorizing them. Try to think of a mnemonic, or memory device, to help your child with the facts he finds most difficult. For example, many children have difficulty with $7 \times 8 = 56$. Have your son write this on a blank piece of paper and repeat it several times until he notes the pattern.

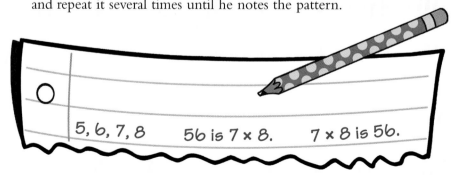

5, 6, 7, 8   56 is 7 x 8.   7 x 8 is 56.

To review facts and identify the troublesome ones, use index cards to make flash cards of all the facts. When your son is unable to recall a fact, make another card with that same fact and add it to the pile. Whenever possible, work with him to devise a strategy to remember that fact.

You might also make a deck of cards to use to practice facts. Make 13 sets of four cards that have the same answer, for example:

2 × 3   18 ÷ 3   3 × 2

36 ÷ 6

Play any of your favorite card games (like War, Concentration, or Go Fish) using these cards. Consider having a family game night and involve the whole family!

These both have the same quotient, so I have a match.

56÷7   48÷6

Q: *With three children in the family, we seem to be always rushing around. How can I find the time to stop and bring out the math in a situation?*

A: Use time that might otherwise be wasted, like the time you spend waiting in line at the restaurant checkout or driving from one place to another. You can also think about math while you are rushing around. Ask questions like these.

- Our check is for $42.50 and, of that, $2.50 is tax. How much should I leave for a tip?

- What do you think will be the total cost of all these groceries?

- How many light-cycles do you think it will take before we get through this intersection?

- How many different ways can three girls sit in the back seat?

- I'm driving 30 miles per hour, how long will it take me to drive four miles?

It seems to be taking about five minutes for each customer to check out. When shall I tell your father to meet us outside?

Thinking About Why Your Child May Be STRUGGLING

I started paying attention in math class, Mom, and now math is a _LOT_ easier!

There can be many reasons why a child may be having difficulty with mathematics. If the child doesn't know what the problem is, trying to figure it out may be like trying to solve a puzzle. If your child is struggling, it is important that you play the role of partner to the teacher.

Thinking About Why
Your Child May Be
STRUGGLING

Q: *My son says he doesn't like math. What should I do?*

A: Nobody likes to fail. Help your child meet with some success. Look in the handbook to find another way to solve problems that are troublesome. Ask lots of questions you know he can answer. Show him he really does know something about math. Talk to his teacher about ways you can help.

Try to be enthusiastic about math. If you didn't like math when you were in school, or didn't do well in math, don't let your son think that makes it OK for him not to try. Do help him see that everyone bumps into things that are hard to do and the best way to get past the rough spots is to spend some time on them.

Use the handbook. You will find the clear, step-by-step approach helpful. Your son should also enjoy the informal style of the handbook. The Math Alerts will help him avoid mistakes before he makes them.

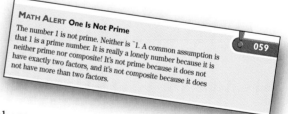

MATH ALERT **One Is Not Prime**
The number 1 is not prime. Neither is 1. A common assumption is that 1 is a prime number. It is really a lonely number because it is neither prime nor composite! It's not prime because it does not have exactly two factors, and it's not composite because it does not have more than two factors.

059

Do not ask him to do pages of drill and practice that have not been assigned in school. That may make him like math even less. If you would like him to practice math at home, use activities and games. Your son's teacher will be able to suggest some good ones. Also, don't forget about board games or card games.

Q: *My daughter seems to have good years and bad years. Sometimes she does very well in math and sometimes she just doesn't do well at all. What might be the reason?*

A: Teachers have different teaching styles, and students have different learning styles. Many children learn best by *visual* methods. Reading about math in a book often works well for these students. Other students learn best by *auditory* methods. They learn most from the teacher's explanation. Other children learn best by *tactile* methods. They need to use real materials that they can pick up and move around. Think about what worked best during her good years, then talk to your daughter's teacher and see whether he or she can find the learning style that works best for your daughter. Then both of you can provide your daughter with help that best matches that style.

> The length is 3 units, the width is 4 units, and the height is 2 units. There are 24 cubes, so, the volume is 24 cubic units.

Sugar Cubes

When this year is almost over, talk to the principal or guidance counselor about your daughter's learning style. These people are aware of the many different teaching styles. Knowing your daughter's learning style will make it easier for them to place her in a math class for the next school year. After a few weeks of the new year, meet with the teacher to discuss whether the teaching and learning styles are a good fit.

Q: *My son doesn't understand the math in his textbook. He needs more hands-on work. How can I help at home?*

A: You can use the handbook to help make math real for your son. You will notice that many of the concepts in *Math on Call* are introduced using a mathematical picture or model. You might try using these models to help your child with topics he is studying in school. For example, cut apart a trapezoid to show that the formula for the area of a trapezoid makes sense. ITEM **368** in *Math on Call* will show you how to do this.

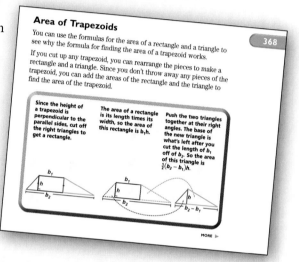

Area of Trapezoids

You can use the formulas for the area of a rectangle and a triangle to see why the formula for finding the area of a trapezoid works.

If you cut up any trapezoid, you can rearrange the pieces to make a rectangle and a triangle. Since you don't throw away any pieces of the trapezoid, you can add the areas of the rectangle and the triangle to find the area of the trapezoid.

Since the height of a trapezoid is perpendicular to the parallel sides, cut off the right triangles to get a rectangle.

The area of a rectangle is its length times its width, so the area of this rectangle is b_1h.

Push the two triangles together at their right angles. The base of the new triangle is what's left after you cut the length of b_1 off of b_2. So the area of this triangle is $\frac{1}{2}(b_2 - b_1)h$.

368

MORE ▶

You will be surprised at how many materials you have right at home that you can use to help your child understand math. When your child is studying surface area, for example, have him cut up used containers from your recycling bin.

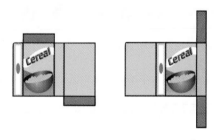

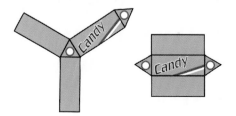

Q: *My daughter does very well on computation exercises, but when it comes to word problems she has a lot of trouble. Do you have some suggestions?*

A: Don't ignore the problem, hoping it will fix itself. First, decide whether she has difficulty understanding what she reads in other subjects. If that is the case, talk to her teacher about ways to improve her reading comprehension.

If the problem is limited to word problems in math, she may need to practice restating a problem in her own words. She may also be having difficulty working through a problem step-by-step. She may be trying to get the answer too quickly. *Math on Call* includes a whole section just on Problem Solving. (See ITEMS 476–494.) Here your daughter can find many problems that have been worked out step-by-step. She should try to imitate the steps when solving word problems on her own.

She may also be unsure when to use each of the basic operations: addition, subtraction, multiplication, and division. When you use each of these operations in your daily life, try to point them out to her.

I am spending money. That's taking it away from the money I have in the bank, so, I need to subtract the amount of that check from my bank balance.

Q: **Sometimes, when my son is working on a new topic, he finds he needs some skills he has forgotten. What can he do?**

A: *Math on Call* can help him here. He can use the handbook either to look up the skills he's forgotten or to look up the new topic. **MORE HELP** references tell where he can go to review the skills he needs.

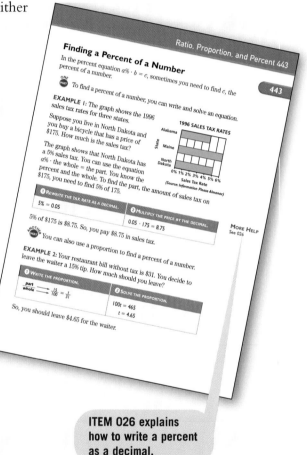

Ratio, Proportion, and Percent 443

Finding a Percent of a Number

In the percent equation $a\% \cdot b = c$, sometimes you need to find c, the percent of a number.

ONE WAY To find a percent of a number, you can write and solve an equation.

EXAMPLE 1: The graph shows the 1996 sales tax rates for three states.

Suppose you live in North Dakota and you buy a bicycle that has a price of $175. How much is the sales tax?

The graph shows that North Dakota has a 5% sales tax. You can use the equation $a\% \cdot$ the whole = the part. You know the percent and the whole. To find the part, the amount of sales tax on $175, you need to find 5% of 175.

1996 SALES TAX RATES

Alabama · Maine · North Dakota

0% 1% 2% 3% 4% 5% 6%
Sales Tax Rate
(Source: Information Please Almanac)

① REWRITE THE TAX RATE AS A DECIMAL.

$5\% = 0.05$

② MULTIPLY THE PRICE BY THE DECIMAL.

$0.05 \cdot 175 = 8.75$

5% of $175 is $8.75. So, you pay $8.75 in sales tax.

MORE HELP See 026

ANOTHER WAY You can also use a proportion to find a percent of a number.

EXAMPLE 2: Your restaurant bill without tax is $31. You decide to leave the waiter a 15% tip. How much should you leave?

① WRITE THE PROPORTION.

part → $\frac{15}{100} = \frac{t}{31}$ ← whole

② SOLVE THE PROPORTION.

$100t = 465$
$t = 4.65$

So, you should leave $4.65 for the waiter.

443

ITEM 026 explains how to write a percent as a decimal.

Q: *My daughter has been having difficulty for several years. She has fallen so far behind that she really doesn't understand any of the math her teacher is presenting. Is there any way she can catch up?*

A: If your daughter's skills are several years behind, she may need some help outside of the regular classroom. You are right that it will be difficult for her to understand the work being taught at her grade level. Talk to your child's teacher as soon as you can. The sooner she is able to receive some extra help, the sooner she will be able to catch up.

Work with your daughter, her teacher, and, if possible, the tutor assigned by the school, to set goals that she can reach. Emphasize the importance of these goals and your willingness to help her attain them.

A: Try to think about what may be going on that is different. Maybe your child needs glasses or a new prescription for his glasses. Perhaps the solution to your problem can be as simple as that.

Your child may have a problem paying attention. Sometimes, as math concepts become more difficult, attention problems can become more obvious. Ask your son's teacher whether he seems to be listening or if something is distracting him. You might want to arrange for your child to sit in a place with fewer distractions, closer to the teacher. If the teacher is aware of the problem, he or she can help your son to focus his attention when his mind seems to be wandering.

Q: *I'm not exactly sure how to approach the teacher. I don't want her to think I am blaming her for my daughter's poor math performance. Should I just wait until she contacts me?*

A: It is best to discuss the problem as soon as possible. The teacher may be waiting until scheduled parent conferences. Meanwhile, the problem is not likely to go away. Also, time is often very limited during a formal conference.

If it is early in the year, the teacher may not be aware of the weaknesses of each student. If you highlight your daughter's difficulty, the teacher will begin to focus specifically on her, and you may be able to solve the problem sooner. There will be almost a whole year to make progress.

When you are ready to speak to the teacher, be sure to make an appointment. Don't try to talk about problems when you are at school dropping off or picking up your child.

The focus of the conversation should be on finding the best way for your child to progress in math. If you concentrate on that and compliment her on things about her class that have worked out well for your child, the teacher will not think you are there to evaluate her performance as a teacher. Listen carefully to how she describes your child. Your daughter may behave very differently at school than at home. You both have a lot to share and together you should be able to work out a plan that will increase your daughter's success in mathematics.

NOTES